Doreen Klahold

Romantic and Realistic Love in Shakespeare's "As You Like It"

GRIN Verlag

Bibliografische Information der Deutschen Nationalbibliothek:

Die Deutsche Bibliothek verzeichnet diese Publikation in der Deutschen National-
bibliografie; detaillierte bibliografische Daten sind im Internet über http://dnb.d-
nb.de/ abrufbar.

Imprint:

Copyright © 2013 GRIN Verlag GmbH
Druck und Bindung: Books on Demand GmbH, Norderstedt Germany
ISBN: 978-3-656-46995-7

This book at GRIN:

http://www.grin.com/en/e-book/230763/romantic-and-realistic-love-in-shakespeare-
s-as-you-like-it

Romantic and Realistic Love in Shakespeare's *As You Like It*

As typical for romantic comedy, the central theme in William Shakespeare's *As You Like It* is love in its various forms. In total, there are four conventional couples (Rosalind & Orlando, Celia & Oliver, Phebe & Silvius, Audrey & Touchstone) and one rejected country fellow (William). Nevertheless, the forms of love differ between those couples. Most of the relationships in *As You Like It* are based on the principle of love at first sight, implying an abrupt and overwhelming falling in love; this can be seen with Rosalind and Orlando right at the beginning of the comedy as well as with Celia and Oliver later in the play, although in the case of the latter the audience does not know at what point of the plot they actually fell in love with each other. An overwhelming romantic, however, is also experienced by Silvius, but his beloved Phebe dismisses him because she believes his love to be a fantasy, mocking thus the principle of love at first sight as well as the impulsive love expressions. In the end, Phebe marries Silvius as she cannot have Ganymede (that is, Rosalind disguised as a man) and, due to this, their relationship can be fairly described as a romantic one but rather as a practical connection. A further type of love is the arranged relation between Audrey and Touchstone, which can be regarded as a parody on romantic love since Touchstone mocks the tradition of courting one's beloved. However, in the last act, Shakespeare unites all different pairs of lovers by marriage, after having compared and contrasted them against each other during the play. Altogether, with this spectrum of love relationships, a greater attention to its romantic expression than to its essence can be found in the play, which shall be analysed briefly in the following.

On one side, the classical literary tradition of love can be found particularly in Orlando's poems and enthusiastic love expressions, until he is educated by Ganymede, as well as in Silvius's courting of Phebe. When seeing her for the first time at court, Orlando is unable to express his feelings: "What passion hangs these weights upon my tongue?" (1.2.236); however, after having reached the Forest of Arden, he begins writing love poems and hanging them on the trees, where Rosalind (already disguised as Ganymede) and Celia (as Aliena) find them: "O Rosalind! these trees shall be my books [...]. Run, run, Orlando; carve on every tree, [t]he fair, the chaste, and unexpressive she" (3.2.5–10). Here we can see that Orlando follows the literary tradition of love when he urges to put his emotions into words and to display them. His poems, despite their poor poetic quality, remind

1

us slightly of Shakespeare's sonnets, for example, Sonnet 130 ("My mistress' eyes are nothing like the sun [...]"), comparing the beloved's beauty to nature:

> 'From the east to western Inde,
> No jewel is like Rosalinde.
> [...]
> All the pictures fairest lin's
> Are but black to Rosalinde.
> Let no face be kept in mind
> But the fair of Rosalinde.'
> (3.2.83–91)

Since Orlando sentimentalizes his experience of love, indulging himself into his feelings, he slightly falsifies his love; the hyperbolism culminates in Orlando's declaration that he will die if Rosalind rejects him. Only through Ganymede's lessons does he then return to the essence and reality of his feelings, noting that dreaming of his love is not enough anymore: "I can live no longer by thinking" (5.2.48). In addition, when Silvius also falls in love with Phebe, he believes his sentiments to be the truest that have ever been: "O, thou didst then never love so heartily!" (2.4.28). Silvius, however, is no poet and does not put his feelings into verse like Orlando does. His expressions of love mainly serve one purpose, namely to convince Phebe of accepting him; whereas Orlando does not directly woo Rosalind but writes love poetry merely for the joy of being in love. Altogether, these have been only a few examples of the literary expression of love in *As You Like It*.

On the other hand, however, there is a more realistic view of romantic love (by Rosalind) and a parody of it (by Touchstone). It is significant that neither Rosalind nor Touchstone tend to express their love in verse; Touchstone only once imitates Orlando's stylistically poor poetry in order to mock the language of lovers. Most of the time, however, when talking about love, they speak in prose, using a realistic and not imaginative language. In this context, Rosalind disguised as Ganymede teaches Orlando to distance himself from the exaggerated romantic love and to return to the reality of everyday life. When Orlando claims that he will die if Rosalind rejects him, she counters down-to-earthly: "But these are all lies: men have died from time to time, and worms have eaten them, but not for love" (4.1.93–95). Furthermore, she considers Orlando's promise to love her forever and a day as false and unrealistic: "Say 'a day' without the 'ever'. No, no, Orlando; men are April when they woo, December when they wed" (4.1.128–9). Similarly, Touchstone underlines in an aside that his intentions towards Audrey are based on his sexual lusts rather than on the wish to build up a lasting marriage, so that "not being well married [...] will be a good excuse for [him] hereafter to leave [his] wife" (3.3.79–80). What is even more, both Rosalind and Touchstone disapprove of the lovers' need to write poetry about their feelings; as Touchstone puts it, "the truest poetry is the most feigning, and lovers are given to poetry; and what they swear in poetry may be said as lovers they do feign" (3.3.16–18). Therefore, there can be seen an obvious contrast between Orlando's and Silvius's expression of romantic love, whereas Touchstone and Rosalind have a more realistic view on it, even though Rosalind in fact somehow enjoys the romantic love of Orlando.

All in all, in *As You Like It*, the focus is laid upon the classical romantic love; but different to some other Shakespearean plays, this literary romantic love is contrasted with a more realistic approach to love. As has been already seen in the few examples above, Orlando and Silvius are the most exemplary characters of romance, whereas particularly Rosalind and Touchstone demonstrate a realistic view on love, courtship, and marriage. However, this does not pose any problems in the relationship between Orlando and Rosalind, because she teaches her beloved how to love in a more realistic way. Touchstone's unromantic interest in Audrey does not deter her either, since Audrey is accustomed to being kicked around by the men. Moreover, Phebe rejects Silvius's advances and romantic love in general until she falls in love with 'Ganymede'; with the help of Ganymede/Rosalind she later accepts Silvius's proposal, but their connection will always be a practical and not a romantic one. Nevertheless, in the end, all relationships – no matter if they are of the romantic, realistic, or practical sort – culminate in the marriage of the lovers, so that Shakespeare does not intend to criticize or devaluate any of them.

Works Cited

Shakespeare, William. *As You Like It.* Ed. R. B. Kennedy, M. Gould. London: Harper Press, 2011.